Jet It, Get It

MW01051392

Jet It, Get It
© 1999 Creative Teaching Press, Inc.
Written by Margaret Allen, Ph.D.
Illustrated by Shelly Hehenberger
Project Director: Luella Connelly
Editor: Joel Kupperstein
Art Director: Tom Cochrane

Published in the United States of America by:
Creative Teaching Press, Inc.
P.O. Box 6017
Cypress, CA 90630-0017

ISBN: 1-57471-416-3
CTP 2906

Bag it.
Box it.

2

Put it in the cans.

Zip it.
Zap it.

Put it in the vans.

Fix it.
Mix it.

6

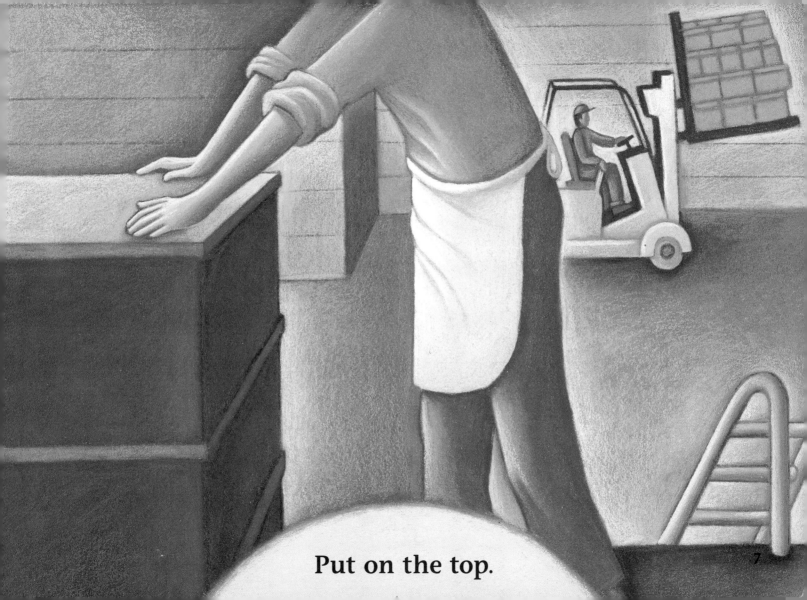

Put on the top.

Mend it. Send it.
Do not stop.

8

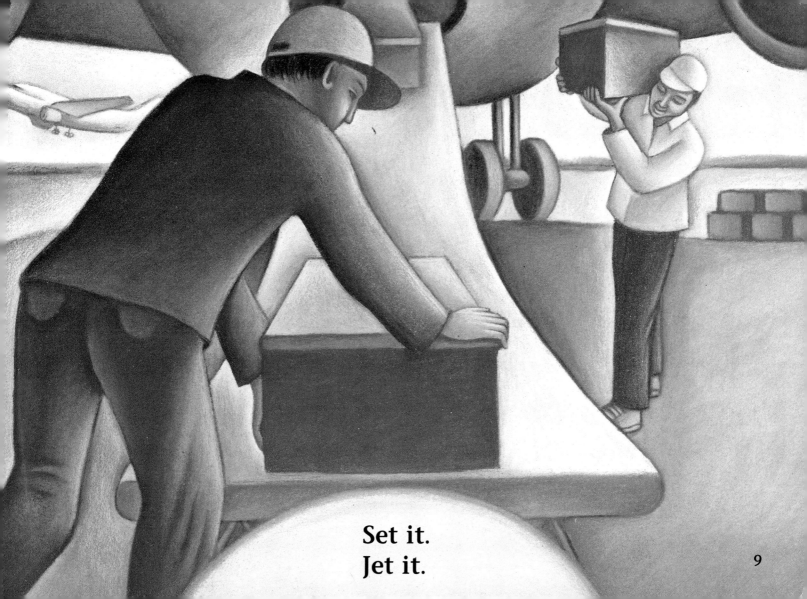

Set it.
Jet it.

9

10

Take off the lids.

Pack it. Sack it.
Get it to the kids.

11

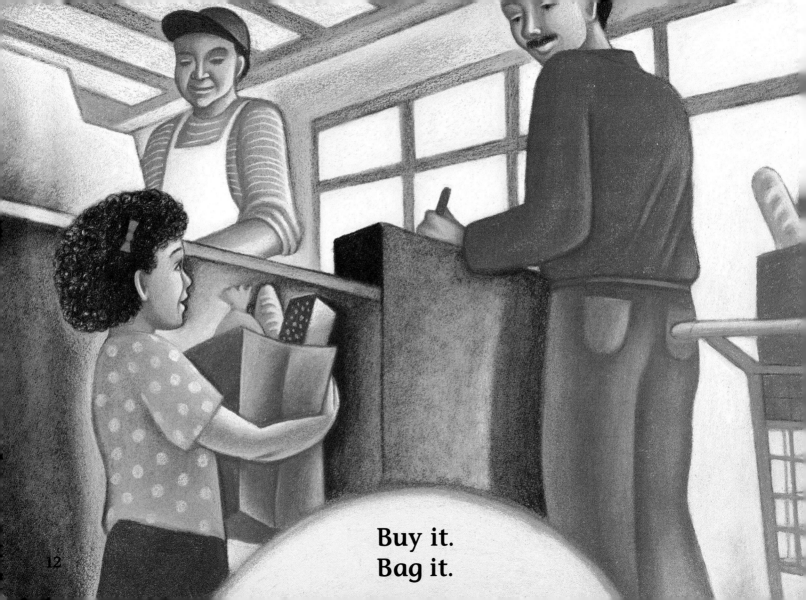

Buy it.
Bag it.

12

Fix it for lunch.

13

Pack it. Snack it.

14

Munch, munch, munch!

15

BOOK 6: Jet It, Get It

Focus Skills: z, x, short e

Focus-Skill Words		Sight Words	Story Words
fix	get	do	buy
mix	jet	for	lunch
box	mend	off	munch
zap	send	take	pack
zip	set		sack
			snack

Focus-Skill Words contain a new skill or sound introduced in this book.

Sight Words are among the most common words encountered in the English language (appearing in this book for the first time in the series).

Story Words appear for the first time in this book and are included to add flavor and interest to the story. They may or may not be decodable.

Interactive Reading Idea

After reading *Jet It, Get It,* play a game called "Zip Zap." When you hold up your hands, have your young reader say *Zip.* Lower your hands and have the reader say *Zap.* Move your hands slowly and have the child articulate each sound as if in slow motion. When you move your hands quickly, the child should say *Zip* or *Zap* quickly. The object of the game is to help your young reader play with the sounds of the words to hear the difference in the vowel sounds since the beginning and ending sounds are the same.